BELONGS TO: __

LEARNING RUSSIAN

Journal and Notebook

Made in United States
Orlando, FL
12 December 2023

40772481R00068